WHO DOUBLED MY PROFIT

WHO DOUBLED MY PROFIT

Ashok Mehta

Worldwide Published by
Pendown Press

PENDOWN PRESS LLP

An ISO 9001 & ISO 14001 Certified Co.,

Regd. Office: 3767A, Kanhaiya Nagar,

Tri Nagar, Delhi-110035

Ph.: 8130886000, 9650072927, 8595249536

E-mail: info@pendownpress.com

Branch Office: 1A/2A, 20, Hari Sadan, Ansari Road,

Daryaganj, New Delhi-110002

Ph.: 011-45794768

Website: PendownPress.com

Edition: 2024

ISBN: 978-93-5554-902-0

Layout and Cover Designed by Pendown Graphics Team
Printed and Bound in India by Thomson Press India Ltd.

Contents

○ ○ ○ ○

Acknowledgements

I am eternally grateful to my parents, who taught me the lessons that have made me who I am today.

Special thanks to my wife, Neetu, and my loving son, Azeez, and my darling daughter, Navya, for their unwavering support and encouragement throughout this journey. Their patience and understanding have been my rock during the writing process of 'Who Doubled my Profit -- Unveiling the Overlooked'.

I would like to express my sincere appreciation to my mentors, guides, publishers, and friends, whose wisdom and guidance have been invaluable in shaping this book. Your insights have enriched every page of this book.

Finally, I am deeply grateful to all my customers for their trust and support, which have been the driving force behind the creation of this book. Their feedback, loyalty, and enthusiasm for my work have been highly instrumental in shaping this book. Thank you for being an integral part of this endeavor and journey."

Last but not least, I beg forgiveness from all those who have been with me over the years and whose names I have failed to mention.

About the Author

As a first-generation entrepreneur in the automotive industry, with over three decades of rich industrial experience in manufacturing automotive differential and drivetrain parts, I am also the author of another book titled "The World Around Axle Shafts."

By education, I am a Chartered Accountant, but my inherent passion for developing new and innovative products and business ideas has made me a Drivetrain Parts Manufacturing expert. I live and breathe drivetrain parts daily, and it continues to remain at the top of my list.

My journey with drivetrain parts began with manufacturing Rear Axle Shafts way back in 1992, but my real entry into drivetrain parts was in 1999 when one of our US performance racing customers fell in love with the quality of our axle shafts and my passion to offer products that no one else was willing to venture into. He made me realize that I had the guts to venture into unknown territories.

Over the years, I've successfully ventured into numerous unknown territories of manufacturing drivetrain parts and helped many small to large customers deliver the parts that solved the problems of their end customers.

When I started my business, I started by making parts that everyone else was making, but over time, the competition sucked all the margins of our customers as well as ours. The root cause was "Yet Another Product" with no innovation, improvement, or value addition.

It used to break my heart to see everyone in our value chain losing, and that is when I decided to create the products and solutions that solve the problems of our customers and their customers.

During the past three decades, I have had the privilege to work with various types of customers. There were those who were always driven by the L1 phenomenon on one extreme, and there were others seeking innovation and product improvement every day.

The journey so far has been brilliant!

○   ○   ○   ○

Who is this Book for?

Written for every business owner, from wannapreneurs to Gen X and CXOs, whether running a start-up or a matured business, no matter if they are catering B2C, B2B, or B2G."

The book is written as a story and takes less than an hour to read, but its insights can last for a lifetime and surely multiply not only your own but also your customers' business and profit phenomenally.

Who Doubled my Profit? is a very simple story through which the author has tried to reveal the profound truths that most business owners overlook and, as a result, keep struggling for profits.

This book is indeed an endeavor to pass on a humble message to those customers who work only towards the lowest prices and overlook the great value their business partner can add.

Without further ado, let's explore these lessons I learned and successfully implemented for and with my valuable customers.

○ ○ ○ ○

Foreword

I first had the pleasure of meeting Ashok in 2015, and from our very first interaction, it was evident that he possessed a unique combination of insight, creativity, and an unwavering commitment to excellence. Over the years, as our paths crossed in the dynamic landscape of business, I witnessed firsthand Ashok's remarkable ability to break down complex challenges, uncover hidden opportunities, and transform them into tangible results.

What sets this book apart is its refreshingly practical approach in the form of stories through metaphorical characters, free from jargon and convoluted theories.

Instead, Ashok offers clear, actionable strategies through real-life experiences that any business leader, regardless of industry or scale, can implement to add value and enhance their bottom line, empowering readers to identify overlooked opportunities and unlock the full potential of their businesses.

The book is all about changing the traditional mindset of "Business is all about saving costs" to "Business is all about adding value and increasing profits"

Throughout the pages of this book, Ashok's passion for helping others succeed shines through, offering a guiding hand to entrepreneurs and executives alike as they navigate the challenges of the modern business landscape.

"Who Doubled My Profit" is not just a book; it's a manifesto for change—a call to action for those who refuse to settle for mediocrity and instead strive for excellence in all aspects of their professional endeavours. Ashok's insights are not confined to boardrooms or corner offices; they resonate with anyone seeking to make a meaningful impact in their industry and beyond.

As you embark on this transformative journey through the pages of "Who Doubled My Profit," I encourage you to approach it with an open mind and a willingness to embrace change. Within these words lie the keys to unlocking untapped potential, doubling profits, and ultimately, reshaping the future of your business.

It's with great pleasure and anticipation that I introduce you to this remarkable work by a truly exceptional individual, Ashok Mehta.

Shiva Menon

Director - Driveline Business Unit

Dorman Products

Who Doubled my Profit?

Once, long ago in a country far away called "Liberty Land", there lived six businessmen. On the other side of the continent, known as "Hindesia", there lived another businessman named **"Ash"** who was a common thread between all six businessmen in Liberty Land.

All six businessmen of Liberty Land ran an automotive products business, and Ash was a vendor to all of them. Each of the six had strong desires to grow their business multifold, had varied ideas to do so, and were in different phases of their economic status when they met Ash to discuss initiation of business.

Ash was initially a very small manufacturer of only one product, but he had a vision to make a name in the industry. He had a passion to accept challenges and create new products, and he never wanted to grow vertically as everyone else in the industry was doing. Ash was a very strong believer that **"Yet Another Product"** would never help him get any closer to his vision.

His biggest weapon to play was to be **Valuable** to his customers, and with everyone selling the same product, the only weapon one can use in the battleground of business is price reduction.

This story begins at a time when the fax machine and telephone were the primary modes of communication. Printed Yellow Pages and newspapers used to be the medium of advertisement.

REPUTATION

Chapter 1

The first businessman was **"Grey"**, who used to be a big customer of the type of products that Ash used to make. When Grey met Ash, he was quite dissatisfied with his vendors as he was not getting consistent quality products and faced regular warranty issues. As a result, he kept changing vendors, eventually connecting with Ash during this process.

Ash received a beautiful sample, and Grey expected Ash to make another sample with the same finish and quality. Although Ash had never made a similar product, he accepted the challenge and managed to create a sample within 40 days, which he then sent to Grey.

Upon receiving the sample, Grey was really impressed and immediately sent it to his laboratory for inspection. Within 5 days, Ash received a phone call from Grey, informing him that he had sent three more products from the same family and had opened a letter of credit for a full container load shipment worth $48,400.

Ash couldn't have been happier because this was the biggest single order he had received at that time, and it was from a big customer in Liberty Land. What's more,

Grey and Ash had never met in person, let alone visited each other.

While Ash was manufacturing the first order, Grey had sent seven more products for a quote, and before the first shipment could move out, Ash received another letter of credit from his bank, which mentioned that the previous letter of credit amount had been increased to $250,000.

As much as Ash was thrilled, he went into a state of doubt because this customer had never met Ash nor seen his manufacturing setup. How could someone trust him so much without even meeting him? Even Ash had never visited Liberty Land. Somehow, Ash went to his bank and enquired if there was any possibility of this letter of credit being fake, and the bank said no.

Somehow, the first shipment left, and while it was still on the water, Ash received another letter of credit from the bank. This time, it stated that the letter of credit amount had been increased to half a million dollars. Ash was absolutely confused, thrilled, but shocked. Thrilled because he had never seen such a big letter of credit in his life, and shocked because it was coming from a customer he had never met. Ash somehow gathered the courage to clarify his doubt with the customer.

Ash called Grey that evening, and here is how that conversation went:

Hi Grey, thank you for this Letter of credit for $500,000, and a big thank you for showing so much faith in me, as we haven't even met so far, and you haven't even seen my setup. Honestly speaking, I am extremely confused right now, and I thought it would be best to call and clarify.

Tell me, Ash, what's on your mind?

Grey, are you aware that I could fill your containers with stones and negotiate the letter of credit for half a million dollars? You haven't met me, and you haven't even seen my first shipment. How can you trust me so much?

Ash, do you think I am a fool sitting here and doing so much business? I have a very old vendor in your country, and I asked him to enquire about you. He has a relative living in your city who knows you well. He has informed me that I can blindly trust Ash.

In Grey's words, Ash found not just affirmation but validation—a validation of his ethos, his integrity, and his unwavering commitment to excellence. The revelation brought tears to Ash's eyes.

The first thing he did upon reaching his office was to inscribe a mantra upon his writing board—a mantra that would guide him through the maze of business dealings, a beacon of light amidst shadows of doubt.

YOUR REPUTATION TRAVELS MUCH FASTER THAN YOU

START
STOP

Chapter 2

The second businessman was **"Lym"**, a seasoned mechanic who found himself grappling with the quality of parts supplied by his local distributor, Mark. These parts, primarily sourced from overseas, particularly a country known as "Chengesia," fell short of Lym's expectations.

As a mechanic, he could discern that the quality of the parts he purchased from Mark was not as good as he had expected. He used to highlight various problems that he faced at the time of fitting of the parts, issues related to durability, and product aesthetics concerns to Mark, and used to suggest various solutions through the ideas he had in his mind.

He had a strong feeling that if Mark implemented any of his ideas, it would greatly help in product improvement and allow both to make extra profit, but unfortunately, he never saw any improvement and finally got frustrated.

Lym's frustration finally started pulling him towards starting his own distribution business. He was seeing a huge business opportunity, and he started imagining creating a big business empire.

He started searching for some vendor(s) who had the caliber and willingness to develop parts. Being a startup, he had limited money and a fear of parts failing, so his search was also for a vendor who could accept small batch quantity. He also had no product design capability, and hence his search was also for a vendor who also had product design capability and the ability to understand what he was drawing on tissue paper or describing and create a unique product out of that.

Somehow, he had this feeling that he could find the quality he desired in another, not-so-well-known but potentially significant Asian country named 'Hindesia'. He started his search for some suitable vendors in Hindesia and came across two vendors named "Siro" & "Gene".

Gene was a major player in the OEM industry, while Siro was comparatively much smaller. Lym was delighted when both agreed to manufacture parts for him. He assigned one part family to Gene and another to Siro. However, Lym ended up having to do a lot of follow-ups with both vendors, and after 9 months, Gene managed to produce a good sample, but Siro was nowhere close. Lym was quite disappointed, as for him, it was a loss of business opportunity with each passing day.

Somehow, the vendor 'Ash' came to know of this business opportunity while he was on a business visit to

Liberty Land. He went to meet Lym. Ash was relatively small in size, but his greatest qualities were his passion for creating something new and challenging, his strong customer-centric approach, his ethical practices, his innovative and progressive mindset.

Lym had big doubts about the capabilities of Ash, as his plant size was way too small as compared to Gene and even Siro, but somehow Ash convinced him to give one chance. Ash was handed over an OE sample and given a challenge to develop a part of the same quality and aesthetics in 35 days, as Lym was personally visiting Hindesia to make sure that Ash did not disappoint him like Siro did.

On the 35th day, Lym visited Hindesia and was happy to see his parts developed at Gene. The next day, he visited Ash's plant, and the first thing he noticed in Ash's room was a writing board with the following quote written on top.

START IS THE BIGGEST STOP

Chapter 3

This was the most famous line of Ash, and he wanted Lym to read it first to remind him that every journey begins with a single step, and that the courage to start is often the most formidable barrier to overcome.

Ash took Lym to another room, and Lym's eyes couldn't believe to see 5 similar parts lying on a table, and Ash challenged him to identify the sample he had given to Ash. This was a 'Flash Light Bulb' (FLB) moment for Lym. He took 20 rounds across the table, picked up and rotated every single part to identify his sample, but couldn't make it out. He then took the parts to the lab, passing through the overly crowded small factory of Ash, and after 3 hours, he returned to the room and surrendered. He had forgotten the fact that Ash's factory was way too small and hardly had any space to move properly through the aisles.

The body language of Lym had completely changed; his eyes were full of excitement and determination as he could see a ray of hope towards the fulfillment of his dreams. Suddenly, he got up from the chair and left his mark on Ash's writing board, proclaiming his faith in Ash.

ASH,
YOU ARE MY MAN!

―― • ● • ――

IT'S THE FIRE WITHIN THAT MATTERS AND NOT THE SIZE

―― • ● • ――

Chapter 4

Lym finally sat down with Ash over dinner and started discussing some product improvements he wanted. While discussing, he took out a tissue paper from underneath his dining plate and started drawing some rough sketches to express what was in his mind for an improved product. To his surprise, Ash could visualize a clear picture of what Lym wanted. Ash promised to make the new part as Lym wanted within the next 7 days. Lym could see his dreams becoming a reality, and Ash could see the excitement in Lym's eyes.

The following day, Lym visited Siro's facility where he observed Siro and his team struggling to produce the part. He was so disappointed that he called Ash immediately, told him that he was canceling his order with Siro, and asked if Ash would be keen to make these parts. Ash agreed, and within 2 days, the 4 new samples were delivered to Ash.

Ash successfully developed the new and improved parts as per Lym's specifications, earning Lym's trust and confidence. While Lym kept buying his first set of products from Gene, he could not see Gene's team enthusiastic about developing more, as they were accustomed to big and regular monthly business volumes from OE customers.

Lym received a very good response from the market, and he continued to send more parts of that family to Ash, resulting in smooth progress. Lym then decided to add more challenging part families to his range and started searching for vendors in Hindesia. However, very few showed interest, and finally, the denials from some became an opportunity for Ash. Lym approached Ash with this new family, and Ash became excited to see those parts. Without even having a very clear idea of how this part family would be made, Ash accepted to manufacture them. In fact, Lym wanted his own improvement ideas to be included, making the product even more challenging. Despite this, Ash accepted the challenge and the order at whatever price Lym offered.

The fact was that Lym had little hope of Ash being successful in this project, but he had already exhausted the options after being denied by other vendors.

Ash did some deep research on manufacturing processes, sat down with a few designers of the industry and other industry friends, and started developing the parts. The challenge did not end here. The material that Lym wanted Ash to use was very expensive and not being produced by anyone in Hindesia. One manufacturer agreed to make it, but only for a very high minimum order quantity that was as big as 11 times the first order requirement of Lym with a 30% payment advance and balance before delivery.

Ash was fully excited to make this new part and accepted the order terms. Another exciting fact was that until then, no one in Hindesia or Chengesia was making that part family, and Ash wanted to be the first to do that.

It took six months of real hard work and investment to make the first samples, and when Lym visited Ash this time, he was amazed to see the product in his hands. The part was 80% right, and Lym gave some suggestions for improvement, but at the same time, Ash could see the eyes of Lym popping out on seeing the real product in front of him. He could see the success almost close and was visualizing the huge profits he would make by selling this profit.

When Lym was sitting down for lunch at Ash's office, he was curious to understand how Ash managed to develop this part when he knew nothing of this part or its materials. Whatever Lym gathered from these discussions, he couldn't resist getting up from his chair right in the middle of his lunch to summarize on the writing board.

CONVICTION PROPELS BOLD DECISIONS FOR SUCCESS

Chapter 5

• • •

Ash took two more weeks to make the improvements, and when the shipment reached Liberty Land, Lym could not believe the positive response he received from the market. His products started selling like hot cakes, and within one month, Ash received a big repeat order for these parts.

While Lym was enjoying the great business he was building, one fine day, Ash received a call from Lym expressing his displeasure over the deliveries from Gene and asked Ash to enquire if there was any problem with them. Ash made some enquiries through internal sources and came to know that Gene's orders from OEMs had grown beyond their current capacity. In view of the pressure from their OEM customers, they had put the aftermarket customers on the back burner. Lym verified this at his level and finally called Ash again to pick up the Gene project as well. Ash quickly developed those parts and helped Lym reinstate his supply chain.

While all this was happening, one day, Ash started thinking while sitting alone in his office. Luckily, Ash could come to the rescue of Lym out of this situation, but what would happen if Lym had to start the work of shortlisting the vendor from scratch?

What would happen if Lym's reliability of Gene was for many parts? Just imagine this situation had happened, then try to answer this question.

Lym would be out of stock for at least 6 months, and his customers would move to his competitors.

His vendor was not affected as he had additional business from his OE customer.

Thinking further, his thoughts went into the root cause of why Gene stopped his supplies while there was no quality or payment issue. After a lot of thought, he realized that Lym's business or market was not the core business of Gene. Whatever had happened in terms of their business dealings was either a trial for Gene to see if he could support such markets or a decision made by Lym when he had no other vendor or did not perceive the risk of working with a vendor whose focused customers / market was different from what Lym served.

The realization became a life lesson for Ash that he got up and wrote on his writing board.

SELECT VENDORS WHO VALUE YOUR BUSINESS

Chapter 6

While Lym was enjoying his new business, there were others in Liberty Land who were watching the speed at which Lym had started growing. One of those was named **"Ray"**, who was working as a technician in an automotive parts company and decided to start a distribution business.

Ray had a particular product design that was unique and intricate, and he had a strong feeling that this product, if made right. would help him establish his new business.

He came across a manufacturer from a country called Suwan who made a part that looked similar to what he wanted, but it was not of the quality he desired. Through a reference from a friend, Ray came across Ash. Ray showed him the drawing he made and the one he received from a vendor in Suwan. Ash understood the specific usage Ray intended for this part and realized that it required special raw materials and heat treatment to make it suitable for the racing vehicles to whom he wanted to sell.

While Ray was happy with the confidence of Ash, his next problem was that he did not have the money to pay, as he had used his savings to buy parts from Suwan. Somehow, he found a partner named "Day" who agreed to invest.

Within three months, Ray had the product he wanted to launch in his hands, and this product was exactly what he wanted. For Ray, the success of this product was very important, as if it failed this time, he would be back to his job.

He took the part to his racer friend, who installed the part in his race car that was getting ready for a race next weekend.

Ray was sitting at home, keeping his fingers crossed on the race day, and suddenly his phone rang. It was his racer friend calling,

"Hey Ray, congratulations! I won the race, and the guy who was ahead of me lost because the part installed in his car failed. Thank You so much, Buddy. It's time to celebrate."

Ray couldn't believe that he was out of stock within the next 3 days and had made a huge profit on that part.

On Wednesday evening, he called Ash and said,

"Thanks buddy. You saved me and made me a successful entrepreneur. I am out of stock in three days and sending you my repeat order. I also have some more ideas that I want to share with you. Let me send some thoughts to you tomorrow, and then we will talk again"

This was once again one of the proud moments for Ash, and the next morning when he reached his office, the first thing he did was write this on his notice board.

YOU CAN GROW ONLY IF YOUR CUSTOMER GROWS

Idea
help double
conference
union
Join
Alliance
shake team
bussinesswomen
Man
friendship
brainstorming
corporate
Communication
Teamwork
Together
strategy
brainstorming
Job Successful
cooperation
office Man
working
work
"trust"
Group
Action
connection
Businessman
hand
"Contracts"
brainstorming man
success agreement

Chapter 7

During the same time, in his endeavors to grow business in Liberty Land, Ash came across another customer named **"Ron"** who was buying from some vendors in Chengesia.

Ash introduced himself as a Trusted Growth Partner from Hindesia, and upon hearing this, Ron raised his voice and started shouting.

"It is really very hard to rely on you people. Eighteen months ago, I gave some products for development to a vendor in Chengesia on the condition that he would not supply that product to any of his competitors for the next 2 years at least. He developed them quite fast and got the samples approved within 3 months, but I was shocked to find that by the time I received my first shipment, the same product was available with five of my competitors. I did so much hard work in identifying a product and getting the same development to make good profit for me, but here I am fighting with five competitors and now struggling to clear the inventory at a loss to get rid of the product."

Ash kept listening as Ron continued to tell his story.

"Almost a year ago, I identified another product and found another vendor from Chengesia. I assumed that last time I came across some unethical vendor and not everyone is like that. After all, the whole world buys from Chengesia. This time I was quite cautious, and before I could release any

information, I asked that new vendor to sign an exclusivity agreement with me. We signed the same, and the part was developed. This time I was quite happy that I would make good profits out of this product, but I was shocked to see the same thing happened in the same way, and I am sitting on the inventory of these parts.

I sued that company, and so far, I have paid more than $100,000 to my attorney, and I don't see any chances. That guy had sold the parts to my competitors from his other fictitious company in Chengesia and has outrightly refused that he has not supplied these parts to anyone in Liberty Land.

Now here I am sitting on inventories and further draining $100,000 as legal fees. I just don't want to take this headache, and I am better off buying my products from Liberty Land instead of wasting my time and money with unethical suppliers."

Ash silently kept listening to all this, and before he could start his sales pitch or share with him how trustworthy he was, Ron outrightly told him that he is currently not in a state of mind to buy from overseas and asked Ash to leave.

Ash realized that this is not the right time and left Ron's office.

While on his way back, he was trying to recollect the whole sequence of events that Ron explained and started asking what could happen if Ron had come across a vendor who was ethical.

Ash came back home and wrote on his writing Board.

CONTRACTS MATTER BUT TRUST MATTERS MORE

Chapter 8

A few weeks passed, and while Ash was sitting in his office, he suddenly received a call from the courier company stating that they had a delivery from Liberty Land that they wanted to make. While Ash was expecting another sample of the parts that he was making, to his extreme surprise, he saw the courier company arriving with half a truck load of samples sent by Lym. It has 70+ samples that literally filled half of Ash's room to the roof. Before Ash could open these samples, he heard a highly excited voice from Lym over the phone saying,

"Ash, I am really very happy with the dedication and hard work that you have put into my parts, and I want to keep you so busy that you don't even think of going to someone else. Here are some samples of nine different families, and I want you to make all of these, and I am very confident that the way you could make the recent parts, you will make these as well".

Ash was in a state of shock and did not know what to answer. After the call was over, he got up from his chair and wrote the following on his writing board.

○   ○   ○   ○

CHALLENGES MET WITH DEDICATION = FULFILLING REWARDS

Chapter 9

It took two full days to open all the samples and ten more days to categorize them into different families, and probably months and months to understand their applications and how they would be made. The majority of these part families were unknown to the people of Hindesia, as most of them were meant for some sort of racing applications.

Lym's expectations on these parts were to use these parts for benchmarking purposes, primarily focusing on their sizes. He wanted Ash to reduce the weight of some parts by using alternate materials or by removing weight from unwanted areas while maintaining strength. Additionally, he wanted Ash to use much stronger materials and special strengthening techniques so that those parts could withstand the rigors of racing, among other requirements. Each part family had its own unique requirements and challenges.

As much as Ash was super excited to see these new parts and the faith that Lym had bestowed on him, he was equally burdened and having sleepless nights on the other side. This was quite a big challenge for Ash to accept. This was an unknown territory for him, and the expectations were quite stringent.

One of those days, Ash was sitting with his mentor, "AY", and discussing this situation. AY, the mentor, kept listening for two hours and kept probing him in different ways to understand how he was feeling. Finally, Ash shared his fear of failure. He did not want to tarnish the good image he had created in front of Lym.

At that moment, AY asked Ash to think of the biggest fear of his life and magnify it by 20 times. Once Ash reached that peak, AY asked him how big the fear of failure was as compared to the magnified fear he saw.

Ash understood the message loud and clear. He opened his eyes and went straight to his writing board to inscribe his latest learning.

KILL YOUR FEARS AND REDEFINE LIMITS

Chapter 10

He immediately opened his computer and wrote to Lym.

LET's GO

Ash started picking the products one by one. He started learning step by step and realized that whenever he picked a product, the whole universe conspired to help him. Sometimes he would sit in front of a part for hours, visualizing how it could be made. Once that was sorted out, the next challenge would be learning about alternate materials, manufacturing processes, and finishes that would meet Lym's stringent requirements. Another big challenge was that each product would require the acquisition of one or more new machines. Arranging raw materials was always challenging due to small batch sizes and inconsistent order frequency.

The journey was, of course, very challenging and full of roadblocks, but this was the least expected when he had decided to enter an unknown and difficult terrain.

Whenever Ash would start feeling low, he used to recall what his mentor had mentioned when they sat together last, and that used to change his energy levels drastically. He decided to write this on his writing board.

WHEN YOU BREAK ROADBLOCKS, YOU BECOME A BLOCKBUSTER

Chapter 11

• • •

Every time Ash would deliver a product, Lym saw another success, and by now, Lym had eaten a lot of market share from Mark. Mark got worried and started searching for Lym's vendors.

Ash was participating in an exhibition in another far-off country where Mark could see the products he was searching for at Ash's booth. After discussions, he realized that Ash was the main vendor of Lym. After a few minutes of enquiry, Mark asked Ash,

"Do you know I am the biggest distributor of these parts in Liberty Land?" and Ash's answer was,

"Yes, I know, Sir. How can I help you?" Mark further asked,

"Do you have any exclusivity agreement with Lym" and Ash said,

"No Sir".

Mark's immediate reply was, "I can give you three times more business than what you are getting from Lym, but you have to stop selling to Lym." To this, Ash replied,

"Thank you so much, sir. I am happy you liked my products so much, and your offer is also very generous, but my ethics do not allow me to leave my customers for extra bucks. I am happy with his 1/3rd business."

This was the happiest moment in Ash's life when he realized what his hard work on these products could achieve.

Fortunately, Ash was to meet Lym that day for dinner. Ash shared all the above with Lym, who was also very happy because this was great feedback for him too. He then showed Ash the screensaver of his cell phone displaying the number "51", and he told me this is the market share I want to have for these products.

For Ash, nothing could be more rewarding than this trip. These learnings on the board became engraved in Ash's mind and became his guiding principles.

BECOME A TRUSTED GROWTH PARTNER ~~VENDOR~~

Chapter 12

During this period, another growth-aspiring customer, "Bro", from Liberty Land, came across Ash. Bro had a very small setup, and he used to resell products after buying them from distributors, but he was highly customer-centric and always knew what his customers wanted.

Bro had no experience of imports, and when he met Ash, he shared the types of issues his customers were facing, how he wanted to serve his customers relentlessly, and his aspirations to grow. Ash could see all the traits of being a great entrepreneur in Bro, and somehow Ash decided in his mind that he would help this customer.

Ash told Bro that he would get the parts on a door delivery basis, as if he were getting the products from his distributors, and Bro need not get involved in the complexities of imports, customs clearance, brokers, and local deliveries. The whole idea was to give a trouble-free and seamless service.

Bro, being closely connected with customers, would generally come across new ideas for product improvement or new products, and Ash would take over. His customers were liking his products, and several times the demand for his product would outgrow the inventory he had planned.

Once, Bro called Ash at night when he was about to sleep, informing him of his stock-out situation and requesting to make some parts within days and send them by air. Ash was equally customer-centric, and his response was, "I will grow only if you grow."

In the morning, when he told his plant team about this urgency, the plant team came back saying that the raw material required for those parts was not available and the supplier was promising delivery after 30 days. Ash immediately searched his stock of raw materials and found one that was of a higher grade and hence much more expensive. Ash advised his team to use that raw material and make the desired parts within 72 hours. "If our customer wants the parts by air, then that means our end customers are loving our products, and how can you put a price tag on love?" A special setup was arranged for those parts, and this batch was produced within 48 hours. Bro was astonished to see the parts delivered to his door within 7 days of his requisition. Ash never even informed Bro that he made a loss in this order and never asked for any special premium.

During those days, Bro found a great opportunity with a new product that was developed, and a small batch was tested in the market and received good responses with few minor changes. Bro placed an order for a large quantity. He had advertised well for that product and had very high hopes for its sales.

The day the shipment reaches Bro, Ash gets a call from Bro at night, informing him that there is some problem with the part he received. He explained that the mistake was very small, but unfortunately, none of the products could be used. The order value was quite big, and Bro was worried because he had very limited stock left from the previous shipment. Additionally, he was concerned that Ash might start finding faults in the changes Bro had proposed, but Ash's team misunderstood and ended up supplying parts that could not be used. Bro was astonished to hear Ash's response over the phone.

"If these parts can't be used or reworked, they are not yours. Please scrap them. You will get the correct parts soon. Let's have a joint call with our engineering team tomorrow and make whatever changes are required."

"But Ash, I don't have enough stock to meet demand for more than 3 weeks, and the new parts will take at least 90 days to reach even if you start making them tomorrow," Bro replied.

"Bro, please be assured that you won't lose sales. We will make the products on war footing and send you enough stock to meet your next 60-90 days requirement by air at our cost."

Bro was astonished to hear this bold statement from Ash when he was expecting Ash to abandon him. Instead, Ash was taking such extensive responsibility that he was willing to bear the cost of air shipment, which was almost as much as the cost of the product itself. This meant that Ash was ready to take almost double the value of the shipment as a loss.

The only words Bro uttered at that time were.

ETHICS ARE EXPENSIVE BUT LAST LONG

Chapter 13

Ash also came across another customer named **"Mac"** from Liberty Land who used to sell parts for special trucks. He wanted Ash to make some parts for special vehicles but wanted the parts to be really strong. Ash visited Mac, inspected the parts, and confirmed his willingness to produce them for Mac.

Ash asked for a good $$,$$$ down payment to start the development, and despite a lot of resistance, Mac agreed. After a few iterations, the samples were sent and approved. The production shipment got ready, and Mac happily paid the balance amount that was in $$$,$$$.

Within 7 days of the shipment reaching Mac's warehouse, Ash received an email full of several pictures showing that the parts were manufactured incorrectly. Ash immediately responded and requested Mac to check the entire shipment and inform him of the number of usable parts. He assured Mac that any unusable parts would be scrapped free of cost. Ash had realized that this was due to a lack of knowledge in an important area.

Within the next 7 days, Mac informed Ash that approximately 75% of the shipment had been rejected, and it was hard for him to believe that Ash was assuring him to replace the parts free of cost.

Ash somehow accepted the loss, and only the good usable parts were supplied. The next time Mac met Ash over breakfast, he narrated what he went through while dealing with them:

He said that when he went to his bank to transfer $$, $$$ to Ash, his banker strongly advised him not to send such a large amount, but when he insisted, the banker told him to consider this money lost. The banker was quite adamant, as he had seen a lot of cases where the business owners from Liberty Land had transferred amounts to such countries and the vendors / suppliers had vanished.

Again, when he went to the bank to transfer the balance $$$, $$$ payment, his banker again advised him by saying that he was committing a big mistake.

The day he saw the rejected shipment, he was almost certain that he had lost a significant amount of money. The loss was big, and why on earth would someone take such a big loss, and that too for a customer whose business isn't going to grow so big for this vendor? He in fact called his banker friend and told him that he had committed a blunder despite the advice.

After narrating the whole story to Ash, the last line he said was quite touching, and Ash felt it was worth etching onto his writing board.

ADVERSITY STRENGTHENS THE BOND OF TRUST

Chapter 14

During this time, Ash started his business relationship with a big customer from Liberty Land called **"DRB"**.

Initially, DRB started their business with Ash with a few simple and regular parts. Six months later, Ash went to the DRB office and had the opportunity to introduce himself and interact with the whole team. While Ash was speaking about his experience and how his passion to develop new and complex parts, work ethics, dedicated team, and customer-centric, and one stop shop approach had helped his existing customers by solving their product and service-related problems and growing their profits.

The whole sourcing team at DRB was listening to the bold statements of Ash, which vendors generally refrain from sharing, to use that silence to their advantage. Ash was probably one of the very few such vendors that the DRB team had come across who was willing to offer a variety of product families, along with solutions that would help them sell more.

The management at DRB was quite happy with the presentation and saw great potential in working with Ash. Ash was supposed to leave within two hours after the meeting, but the meeting lasted a good five hours.

Their Product Manager, "Eve", started discussing certain product ideas where the OE (original equipment) product was failing, and he wanted to offer an alternate product that would solve the problem for a specific category of people. While 'Eve' was sharing his thoughts, Ash started feeling that this customer was genuinely made for him. The product and the materials used in it were far from what Ash had worked on so far. However, being the person he is, Ash agreed to venture into this unknown territory and said YES to the project.

Ash discussed this new project with his engineering team when he returned home, and they were equally excited.

Within one year, that product got such a great response that it became one of the star products for DRB. This success gave great confidence to the DRB team and opened doors for numerous new projects for Ash. Eve was also very happy since it was his project, and he was among the few in the DRB team who saw the potential in Ash and took the risk of awarding this project to him.

This success gave great confidence to the DRB team, and this time, when Ash visited DRB, there were thirteen new products from three different families waiting for Ash to see. Ash again accepted the challenge and picked it up all.

One of the products Eve shared was being outsourced from Chengesia but was being offered to Ash due to major warranty issues. Ash examined the part and proposed his approach to manufacturing it. Within six months, the warranty issues with that product vanished.

There was another product family that was quite complex and required a different set of knowledge, which was not so common. The third product family presented its own set of challenges. Within the next nine months, all these products were developed and released in the market. Each product performed exceptionally well.

The next time Ash visited DRB, Eve showed him an OE product and another one made by one of their competitors.

Eve explained that the OE product always breaks at one point, probably due to some manufacturing defect or a specific weak area. He then showed the competitor's product, where the issue with the OE product was addressed, but it generated another problem / weak spot. The challenge was to create a new product design that would address both issues. Ash accepted the challenge and took the parts back home.

In six months' time, Ash and his team created a new design and shipped a couple of prototype samples. Eve decided to give one of these part to a renowned racing enthusiast and industry influencer. The part was fitted into the vehicle, and the moment the gentleman drove the vehicle, he fell in love with the part. After vigorously driving the vehicle for two weeks, he wrote very positive feedback in his blog post.

The result was that customers did not want to wait, and the entire first shipment of the product had to be shipped by air.

This was indeed a proud moment for Ash because this product family was an uncharted territory for him, yet customers were loving the product.

The DRB team had a different kind of confidence in Ash and wanted to work on products that were game-changers.

The next big project that DRB discussed with Ash was an OE product which had a problem of premature failure due to extreme weather conditions. The challenge was to create a product that could withstand those extreme weather conditions and outperform the OE product. Apart from that, this part had its own manufacturing and testing challenges.

The territory was again unknown and difficult, but Ash once again accepted the challenge. It took him and his team 18 months to design and develop that part, but the day this part was launched in the market, the magic was unexplainable. It took six months of real 24x7 hard work to catch up with the demand and build the expected capacities.

When Ash caught up with the demand of DRB, he could sit at peace and started thinking about the life lessons that helped him build this beautiful relationship. The moment he got the answer, he got up and wrote on his writing board.

BOLDNESS BREEDS BREAK-THROUGHS

Chapter 15

Fast forward a few years, Ash had created a beautiful new office, and the only thing he shifted from his old office were the writings on the board.

Ash was going through the golden nuggets on his writing board and sat down to recall his beautiful journey with these customers.

While being grateful to all the customers who had bestowed utmost trust in him and helped him reach this level, he started recalling and assessing how much value he could provide to his customers.

He found that:

Grey had retired and was enjoying his riches. He was living in a 12-acre mansion and earning a lot through his huge investments made from his business savings.

Lym sold his company to a private equity firm in a multimillion-dollar deal a long time ago and ventured into another business. The home he bought thereafter was valued at $20million.

The business of Ray was growing at a fast pace. Having started from a small rented warehouse, he now owned a 70,000 sq. ft beautiful office & warehouse. Ash has been his Strategic Growth Partner since the beginning of their relationship.

Ron could not recover from the losses he incurred dealing with two Chengesian companies. He went out of business and is now working for other company.

DRB's business grew multifold with Ash. Their business with Ash had grown - >10 times in the last 5 years.

The business of Bro has grown multifold and is now operating out of a warehouse >100,000 sq. ft. Ash has been his strategic growth partner ever since he started importing.

Mac has been a consistent customer and continues to grow his business with Ash.

While the business was growing, Ash wanted to create more value for his customers and started listing down their pain areas.

After deep thought and running through his numbers, his eyes could not believe what those numbers showed. He came to the realization that he could help his customers double their profit. Surprisingly, this was apart from the benefits he had been giving to his customers by working towards their growth, which eventually resulted in his growth.

He created the following message for his customers, which was quite bold and unbelievable, but all it cost was their precious undivided attention for 20 minutes.

<hr>

DOUBLE YOUR PROFIT
IN 1 YEAR & RELEASE
BLOCKED CASHFLOW

<hr>

Write to ASH at -

ashok.mehta@emmforce.com

for an exclusive 20-minute Zoom / Teams meeting to discover:

How we help our customers:

- Double their Profit in one year

- Reduce the inventory holding period by minimum 45 days

- Minimize sales losses due to stock out situations

- Increase their customer retention

- Minimize the risk of their Dead Stocks